Take a Ride on the River

a tour guide
trip on the Colorado
from Glen Canyon Dam
to Lee's Ferry

by

Audrey Lee

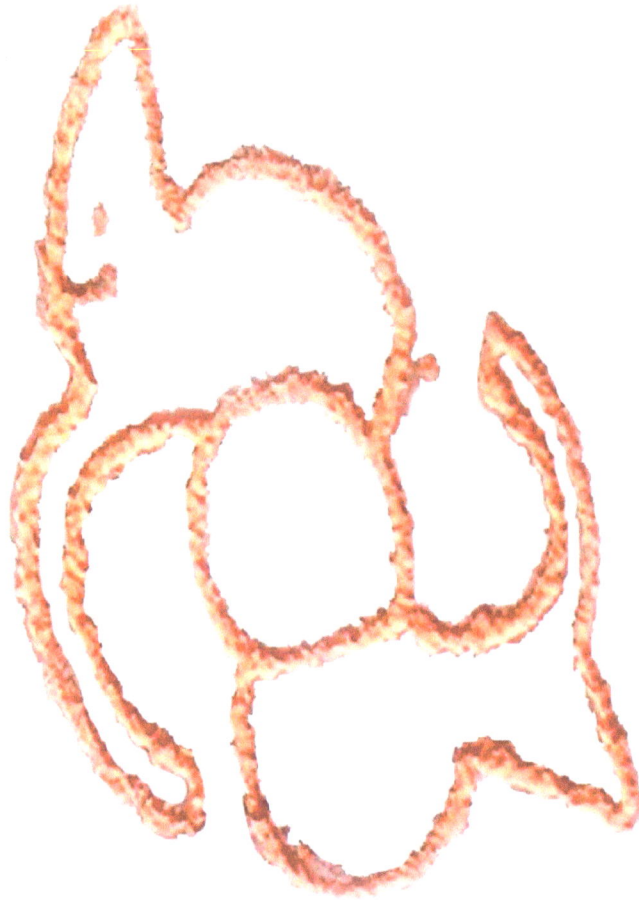

Take a Ride on the River
Copyright © 2011 by Profundities

ISBN 978-0615539959

Printed in USA

www.profundities.net
www.audreyleestoryteller.com
www.onceuponastorytime.net/theriver

It is only in adventure that some people succeed in knowing themselves-in finding themselves.

Andre Gide, Journals,
October 26, 1924,
Justin O'Brien

Introduction

Taking a raft trip down the Colorado has been, for many, the dream of a lifetime. Many have traversed this course, Native Americans, explorers, adventurers, thrill-seekers, and just plain folks like you and me. Vendors have been working with the National Park Service to bring these adventures to the general public since 1968. Included in the exciting activities is a fifteen mile float trip from Glen Canyon Dam to Lee's Ferry. This section of the Colorado is benign, placid and affords a lovely morning or afternoon's getaway to wonders minimally changed from when they were first discovered.

Previously, there has been nothing written for the public to describe and serve as a keepsake of this little jaunt down one of the world's most magical rivers. We will take you on a virtual tour. Hopefully, when you are finished with this tale, you will be "bewitched......to take the Colorado into [your] soul to sing of all that is real."

We thank the National Park Service for their aid, information and support.

Most of all, we appreciate and offer our heart-felt thanks to Claire Gerus for her assistance with editing this manuscript and Barb Anderson at DM Book Pro for her assistance with marketing and publishing.

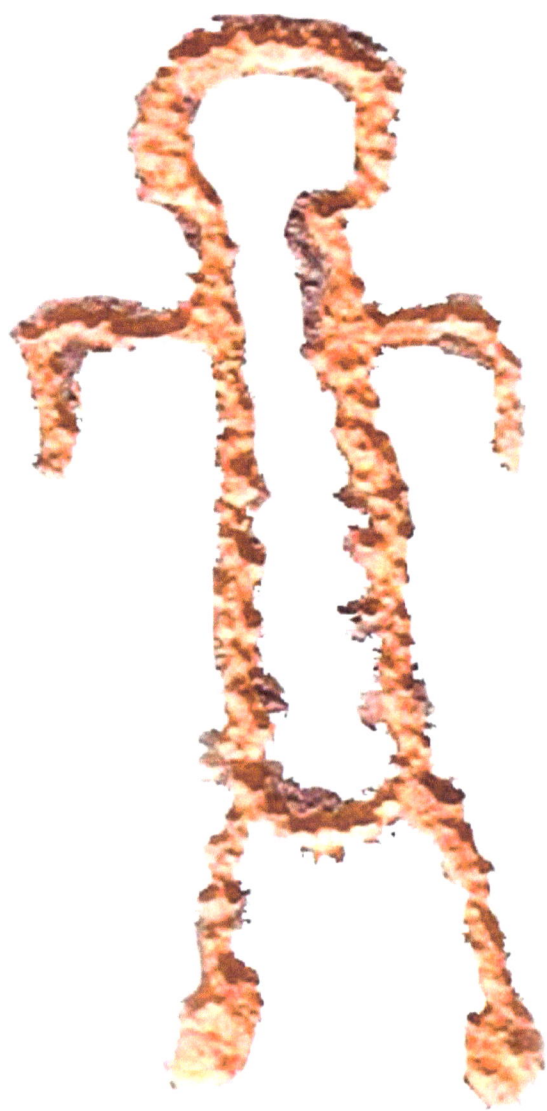

COLORADO

River running through the rock,
determined, as you see,
to carve its pathway deep
    into the belly of earth and stone--
    twisting, turning, raging--
and determined, also,
    to write "Colorado" into the hearts
    of all who ride it--wild and free.

River, coursing through my soul--
entranced, so I feel--
singing its siren's call,
    beating rhythm of water and rock,
    charming, seizing, beguiling--
and bewitching all to
    take the Colorado into their soul
    to sing of all that is real.

TABLE OF CONTENTS

—WELCOME RIVER RUNNERS—

My name is Audrey Lee and I will be your guide to "Take a Ride on the River." I will guide you on a relaxing, awe-inspiring and matchless Float Trip fifteen miles down the Colorado River from Glen Canyon Dam (above) to Lee's Ferry, Arizona. We will talk about our ancestors. Our "ancestors" are anything or anyone who has come before us. We will tell their stories as well as our own. And we will see almost exactly what they saw. We will talk about the changes in the
canyon and how the canyon changes us.

So come with us and become a River Runner for a time. Find out about our ancestor River Runners. We will discuss many things regarding geology, exploration, ecology, history and hydrology. We hope to also open our eyes, ears and souls to the majesty of our surroundings.

The first question to ask ourselves is why do we come? Are we looking for more than just an enjoyable time? Are we open to more? Finally, the real question to consider is: do the people who come here affect this canyon more than it affects them?

One of the greatest changes that man has made to the canyon is the creation of Glen Canyon Dam. Some facts about the dam and bridge are:

The Glen Canyon Dam Project was begun in 1956 by blasting the diversion tunnels through the rock so that the river could be channeled around the riverbed.

The dam is 710 feet high, 25 feet thick at the top and 300 feet thick at the base, the length of a football field. It holds back approximately 27 million-acre feet of water at full pool. Compare this to putting all that water into soda or beer cans and lining them up end to end; this collection would circumnavigate the globe at the equator over 280,000 times.

The bridge was built in Chicago, shipped to Page in pieces, and put together from either side of the canyon like a big erector set. Workers connecting the bridge together at the middle found that the sections met at only one-quarter inch difference. Therefore, the workers named it The Quarter Mile Miracle (the bridge being a quarter of a mile long).

Of course, the dam has changed the river in some ways. However, this Float Trip will differ in very few details from the landscape that the first river runners experienced.

First of all, "Colorado" is Spanish for the color red, which is how the river often looked pre-dam. The reddish coloration was due to the amount of red sand and clay being carried by the river. Today, the river is viridescent, reminding us of liquid emeralds. Actually, the green color is due to the feathery (cladphora) algae, which supplies nutrients for a variety of life forms. Another change is that the river now runs a steady flow between 5,000 cfs (cubic feet per second) and 25,000 cfs to comply with the 1922 Colorado River Compact. This divided the Colorado River users into two categories-upstream and downstream. According to this agreement, the upper states (Utah, Colorado, New Mexico and Wyoming) must release 75 million acre feet of water every 10 years for the use of the lower states (Arizona, Nevada and California). The standard release of water is equivalent to between

5,000 to 25,000 basketballs shooting out of the dam every second. By comparison, before the dam the river's flow varied from a raging torrent to a trickle during periods of drought. Thanks to this regulated release, the residents and visitors to these seven states receive plentiful energy and water that makes living in hot desert areas possible. America as a whole also enjoys the benefit of crop irrigation because twenty five percent of the nation's crops are grown using water from the Colorado River.

Additionally, in 1860, the Tamarisk tree (originally from the Mediterranean, see picture on the left) was planted to mitigate a soil erosion problem.

Since then, they have invaded the entire Colorado River Basin. The Tamarisk crowds out the other plant life, can drink up to 60 gallons of water per day, and is next to impossible to eradicate.

Last of all, the river now flows from deep beneath the warm surface of Lake Powell and maintains a consistent 45 to 50 degrees Fahrenheit coming out of the dam. The plentiful trout fishery made available by this cold water is seen as a benefit by many fishermen. Conversely, the Colorado used to fluctuate from near freezing in the winter to approximately 85 degrees in the summer months.

Other than these few changes, the landscape remains just as it was when the first explorers viewed the canyon. So come with us as we go back in time. And, as honorary River Runners, we will talk about our ancestors. Ancestors are people who have come here before us and have seen these same incredible sights. It is always the question-which influences the other more, the people affecting the river or the river affecting the people? You decide.

As we look at the cliffs, you will see mostly 220 million year old Navajo Sandstone. Later on, we will point out the Kayenta and Chinle shale formations. These three layers are considered the topmost layers of the Glen Canyon system. The geologic formation of Glen

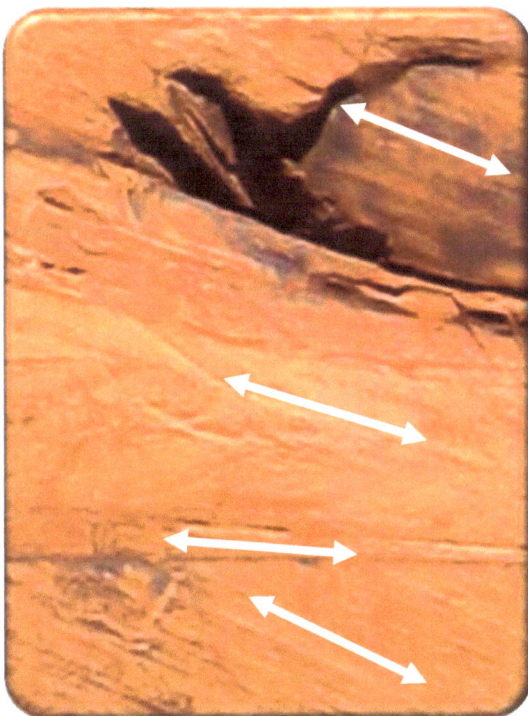

Canyon occurred between 570 million years ago to the last ice age 11,000 years ago. What you are seeing on the face of the cliff on the left is called "cross bedding" (illustrated by the arrows). Throughout most of the geologic record, the Colorado Plateau (a 130,000 square mile area with its center at the Four Corners) was desert with all these hills being sand dunes. At other times, the entire area was covered with the low level, freshwater Cretaceous Sea. The layers that seem to go in different directions are just indications of which direction the prevailing winds were blowing at the time. Actually, sand is simply ground-up clear quartz crystal. Minerals within the sandstone cause the coloration within the rock.

Additionally, the surface of the rock is affected by microbes that take iron oxide and manganese into their systems, mixing the minerals with their body fluids. Then, the microbes excrete the minerals onto the rock creating a form of cement; and with atmospheric changes, the minerals begin to oxidize and change the color of the surface of the rock. It takes up to 700 years for the lighter colors to form, and over 3,000 years for the black to form. This is called Desert Varnish or Navajo Tapestry. When the black develops a highly polished look, it is called Patina.[4]

What were the people like who came here? The archaic desert peoples sought out this forbidding land to call home for reasons of their own. Major John Wesley Powell suspected (from a drawing by a Native American) that it was to escape the greed and religious fervor of the Spanish conquistadors and the missionaries.[1] Our Native American ancestors carved their histories into the rocks and carved their homes into these cliffs. Major Powell came to explore and chart the last remaining unmapped territory in the United States.[1] And why did you come?

Against the wall on the far side of the river, is a basket that is used by Grand Canyon Monitoring and Research Department to get to the center of the river to test the water. This stretch of river runs at 8 knots and is 97% pure. We don't recommend drinking it, however; these days all water should be treated.

Actually, hikers still come down to the River by The Ropes Trail, on the right side of the river, which is actually the easiest hiking trail down into this section of the canyon. Hikers use a cable (formerly a rope, hence the name) embedded in the rock on the steepest decline to get over the slick rock.

To the left, Little Niagara, seepage from the dam, flows from the porous sandstone. Water seepage from around the dam flows at a rate of 2,600 gallons per minute, which is a natural occurrence.

Honey Draw is an excellent example of how rapids are formed. During rains and flash floods, water forces rock and sand through the canyon and deposits them onto the alluvial fan that you see here. As the water pours over it, it begins to boil. The size of the rapid depends on the size of the rocks, sand, flow of water and the narrowness of the canyon. Some people tell the story of a "honey wagon" (sewage collection truck) being dumped here; and, therefore, the name, whether or not this is a true story, is up for discussion.

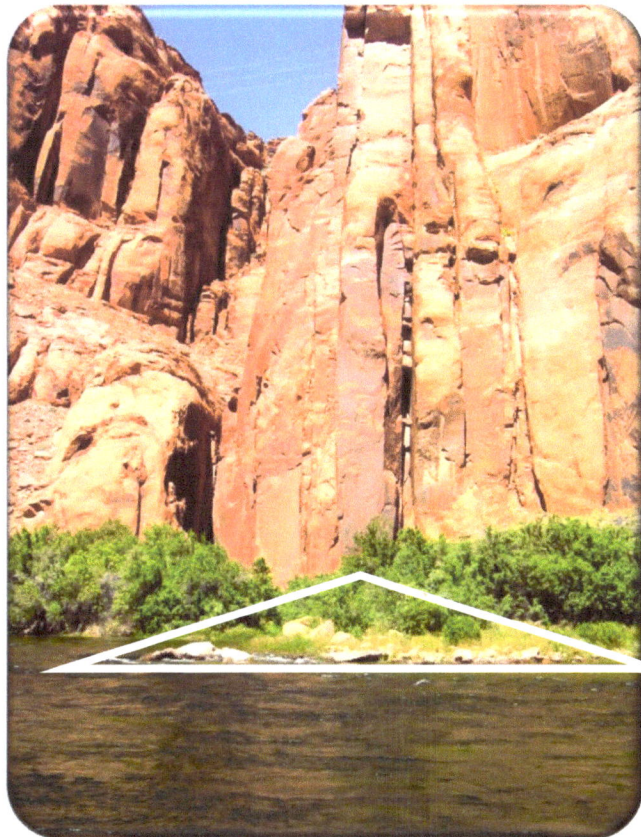

In the past, some rapids were so turbulent that boats flipped on a regular basis. This tendency caused Bus Hatch, one of the first commercial river runners, to comment that the way to run the river was to start upside down. That way, you'd end right side up![2]

One of our first River Runner ancestors was a man named Tio, whom we know about through a Hopi story. Native Americans had no written language and handed their history down through stories told from generation to generation. Tio and his people believed that to go down the Colorado was to go into the belly of the earth where the Spirits dwelled. When his people were experiencing a crippling drought, Tio wanted to appease the spirits and plead for rain. So, he had someone wrap him up in a hollow cottonwood log and throw him into the river. What happened? Unfortunately, we do not know the rest of the story.[2]

It wasn't until 1869 that we had any kind of documentation about running the river.[1] Major John Wesley Powell, a geologist and civil war veteran who lost his right arm in the Battle of Shiloh in the Civil War, went on to fight and then came out West to do all of this adventuring—all with one arm. He was an incredible man who later became the second Director of the Department of Geologic Survey and began what was a precursor to the National Geographic Society. He brought nine men and four boats to start the exploration down the Green and Colorado Rivers. Since this was the last uncharted region of the United States, one of his goals was to make maps of this region; however, he lost most of his instruments to the river, hence his return trip in 1871.

When coming into Glen Canyon Powell writes:[1]

On the walls, and back many miles into the country, numbers of monument-shaped buttes are observed. So we have a curious ensemble of wonderful features- curved walls, royal arches, glens, alcove gulches, and monuments. From which of these features shall we select a name? We decide to call it Glen Canyon.[3]

Major Powell named many things during his expedition, including the rock spire on the right - Monk Rock. Some people think that it looks more like Winnie-the-Pooh or Darth Vader! What do you think?

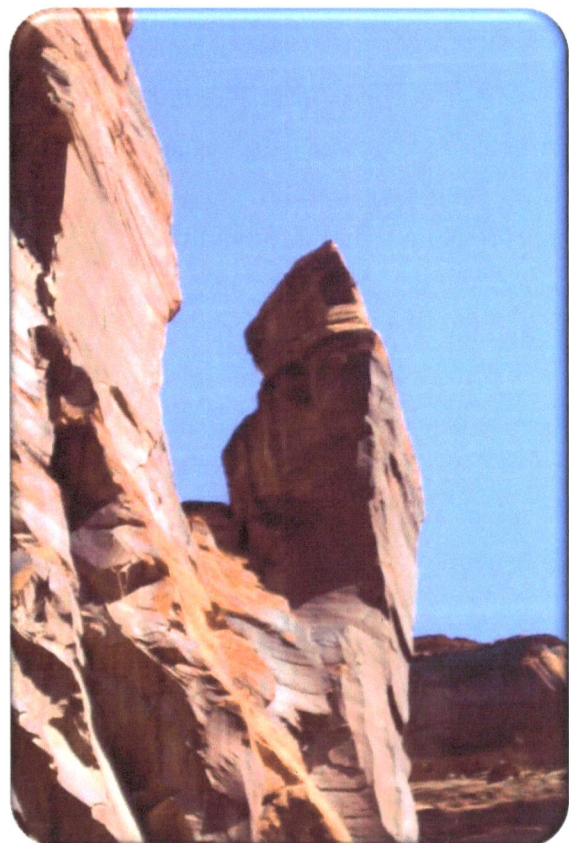

6

Powell had a strong, take-charge nature that caused a rift with three of his men on the 1869 expedition. They eventually hiked out and disappeared. But there were also people who were fond of Powell. One of his men said that Powell could tell a story that hadn't even happened yet! Without a doubt, some of the things that we take with us are stories and memories that will enrich our lives.

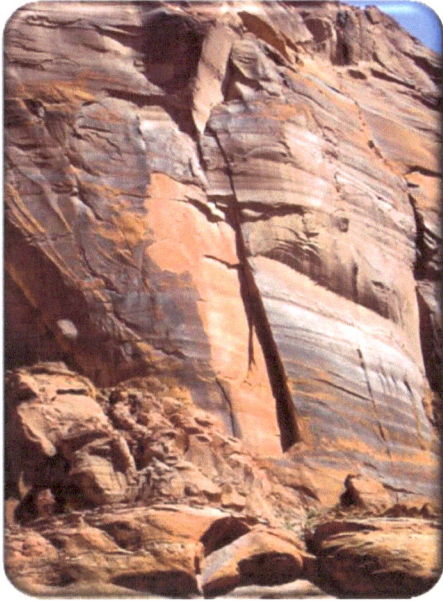

And, of course, we take many more memories with us such as natural "objets d'art" like our Abraham Lincoln Pez dispenser (on the left). If we just use a little imagination, we can see all sorts of creatures and shapes in the rocks. Emerson writes, "There are no days in life so memorable as those which vibrated to some stroke of the imagination." And using our imaginations to see formations in the rocks seems to connect us in some ethereal way to the land.

Again, we ask, "How is this landscape affecting us?"

Below you see Ferry Swale with hanging canyons above. These canyons do not have the flow of water in them that is present in the main channel. The hanging canyons only have a flow of water during rainfall; therefore, the hanging canyons are not eroded to the level of the Colorado River.

The beach at Ferry Swale was also used in the movie, "Broken Arrow," in the scene when Christian Slater and John Travolta came busting out of the mine shaft. We usually see rainbow trout at this beach as well.

Actually, we happen to have a picture of one of the hanging canyons just after a rainfall (see opposite).[1]

Speaking of fish, these fishermen are fishing for trout-mostly for Rainbow Trout but there are Brown Trout present as well. The fishing rules on this river require barbless hooks and no live bait; plus, all fish over 16 inches must be thrown back (this is to keep the breeding stock in the river).

If any of the endangered fish (Humpbacked Chub, Bonytail Chub, Colorado Pikeminnow, Razorback Sucker) are caught, they must be returned to the river. However, these fish need much warmer water than the 45 to 47 degree water in the mainstream of the dammed portion of the Colorado. They need at least a 60-degree water temperature to breed. They will only be found in some of the back eddies or in tributaries such as the Little Colorado.

As you'll recall, some of the rock surface is colored through the actions of a microorganism. Another way that the rock surface can be affected is a process called "spalling." Water soaks into the rock, and in winter will freeze at times, causing some of the surface to pop off as shown in the opposite photo called, "The Lady in the Swing."

Left is the largest example of spalling found in this portion of the river. This large alcove spawl is over 400 feet high, and is called Pacman's Ghost because of the marks within the arch.

On the right, the specimen of Blue Agave (a type of Century Plant), stands approximately fifteen feet high and grows abundantly in Glen Canyon. It blooms once in its five to one-hundred-year life span, and can grow eight to ten inches a day! Once it blooms, it will die. The root of the plant is used to make Tequila.

Left, on the cliff face, is the Steps Trail and what we call Petros Beach. The Steps Trail is named because the cliff side appears to be formed in large steps, and this is the second trail access to the canyon after the dam. It is still used by animals such as Bighorn Sheep. Now, you can see why the Ropes Trail is easier.

At Petros Beach the outhouses are cutting edge technology. The National Park Service installed these Clivus Miltrum outhouses in the canyon for conservation purposes. These $10,000 toilets have a solar panel on the roof, which runs an exhaust fan that extracts all the moisture from the waste below. They do not use any water or chemicals and do not stink.

So, now you will be able to tell your friends that you have seen the best outhouse in the world!

Now, let's go on the petroglyph panel, which is an easy quarter-mile walk from the beach.

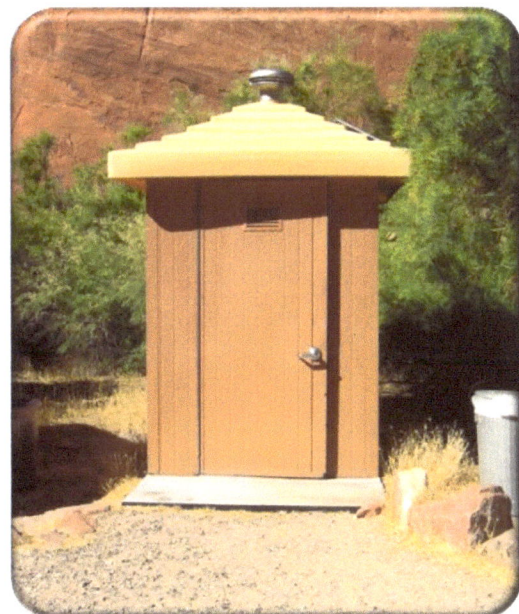

This petroglyph panel is only one of thousands of panels found on the Colorado Plateau. It dates from 9,000 to 1,300 years ago, except for the 'W', done by John Wetherill in the late 1800's or early 1900's. Remember that when we talk about what these drawings mean, it is just educated guessing. There was no written history at the time these drawings were made, so we have no interpretation guides.

The antelope below represent animals that were very important to these hunter/gatherers. More drawings probably lie beneath the sand; however, they remain unexcavated because the National Park Service does not want to interfere with natural erosion.

The 'e' shaped figures are believed to represent water dippers and directions to waterholes.

A large circle with what looks like two heads on either side has been interpreted as a symbol for the Antelope Clan, the Mountain Sheep Clan, the Hump-backed Chub Family, or the birth of twins.

The next grouping may represent a warrior teaching his son or "half-man" to hunt. They may have killed the Mountain Sheep in front of them (the spear in the back and the line underneath the sheep may mean death, see picture opposite).

Due to the patina that has formed over this Mountain Sheep carving, this is one of the oldest petroglyphs on the panel.

With his arms hanging down and his body hollow, this carving might be a memorial for a man after his death. To be on this extensive panel and commemorated this way, he may have been someone very important, possibly, for instance, a medicine man or chieftain.

On the right, we have a carving that may represent the Steps Trail, leading out of the canyon. There is also what seems to be another stair step petroglyph on the panel.

The marking on the far right of this section of the panel, which resembles a thumb, may refer to Tower Butte. The butte stands one mile high on Lake Powell and has always been an important landmark; it is actually quite near the grouping on the left, which may be a hunter with a male, a female and a young Mountain Sheep.

The entire grouping is possibly telling the story that hunters can find mountain sheep in the Tower Butte area.

On the right, we see what might have been meant to tell a story of a birthing scene. This Mountain Sheep is facing to the East, which for Native Americans is the direction of rebirth and regeneration. The center of her body is hollowed out, possibly indicating that she has just given birth to the baby sheep behind her.

And finally, on the left, is possibly a bird of prey, which has been carved, in absolutely elegant symmetry.

A Western Whiptail lizard comes to bid us farewell as we leave Petros Beach.

As we leave Petros Beach, we wonder how this canyon affected the people who carved their stories and lives into the rock, and what other ancestors have seen these carvings. If not the petroglyphs, we know that our ancestors did notice all of the chiseled petrified dunes as well as the crystalline sky. Some were more knowledgeable about the geologic processes, and some had other things to offer.

At this point, as we float down the river once more, I enlist all our River Runners to join me in an adapted version of an old favorite done by Credence Clearwater Revival that seems to aptly fit our journey. Some join in an harmonize, but we all enjoy a loud and even entertaining rendition of the song "Proud Mary," otherwise, more popularly called "Rollin' on the River."

We are now at the top of Horseshoe Bend's curve, which is a 270-degree turn in the river. The boat gives us some idea of the immenseness of it all. The cliffs here are over 1,000 feet high. Actually, the top of the cliff can be accessed from Highway 89 (just a couple of miles out of town at mile marker 545). The contrast of the boat in front of the cliff is a good example of the immenseness of this land. It may be a short ¾ mile walk to the edge, but never do it on a moonless night! It's a long drop down!

Photo Courtesy of Frank Talbott

An abandoned Golden Eagle's nest lies just south of Horseshoe Bend overlook. It is actually as big as our boats, approximately twenty-two feet long and nine feet wide.

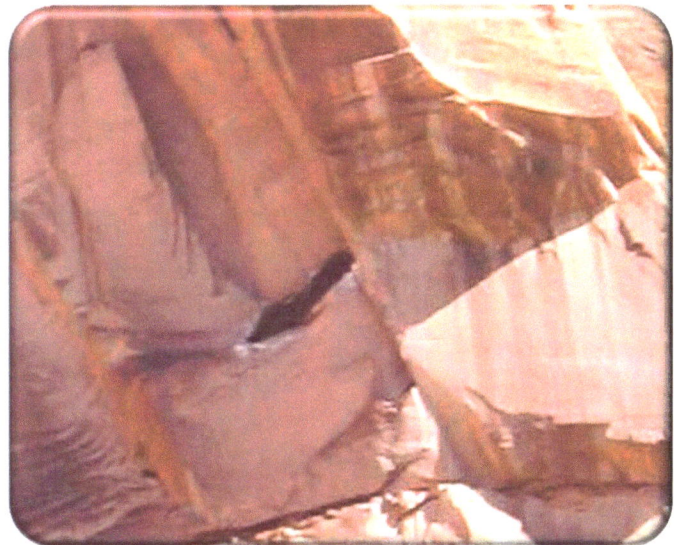

Finger Rock, right, is the most photographed formation on our trip.

On our way to lunch beach, we pass the Praying Hands, which are opposite Finger Rock.

In 1911, brothers Emory and Ellsworth Kolb, made the world's first true-life adventure movie about running the river. Barry Goldwater (river runner number 70) also made a movie, which actually got his political career started.[2]

We also know of Norman Nevills, who "borrowed" a horse trough, wood from his grandmother's outhouse, her curtain rods and Utah highway signs to make a boat and oars. Norman took his wife, Doris, down the river from Mexican Hat, Utah, to Copper Canyon (67 miles downstream) for their honeymoon. Later, after their untimely death in a plane crash, their partners formed the Mexican Hat Expedition Company. Norman's boats were named "What Next," "Don't Know," and "Who Cares."[2]

Glen and Bessie Hyde also came to the Colorado River for their honeymoon. They made it to Phantom Ranch, which is about 100 miles from here. However, their boat was found beached on a riverbank further down river, and the couple had vanished. Since they had a disagreement about returning to the river after they had resupplied on the rim above Phantom Ranch, the mysterious disappearance of the Hyde's is yet another story told and retold on the river.

Much speculation has occurred over the years regarding their disappearance. No one knows if they drowned, tried to hike out or starved. Indeed, twenty-five years later, when the story was told around a river trip campfire, one woman piped up, "I know what happened. I'm Bessie! I shot the S.O.B.!"

However, after testing, she was proven an imposter. But the mystery still had another twist. After the death of Emory Kolb, famed Grand Canyon photographer, at whose studio Glen and Bessie had had their picture taken, a male skeleton with a bullet hole in his skull was found in the attic of the his studio. Initially, people wondered if this was Glen. But again, DNA proved this theory in error.

There were also rumors that one of the most famous River Runners, Georgie White, "The Woman of the River," was the infamous Bessie Hyde. Again, however, testing put the lie to this rumor. Actually, Georgie began running the Colorado with Harry Aleson in life vests in 1945. Georgie's second husband, James White, accompanied her once in awhile; however, his role (given his profession as a truck driver) was usually transportation of people, supplies and boats.

On one trip, they used a 3-foot by 6-foot rubber raft that they could barely fit into. Harry and Georgie kept hiking and rafting in the Grand Canyon until people began to view Georgie as an expert. In 1950 she was invited to be a chaperone for starlets in the movie, "River Goddesses." While rescuing the young actresses from all sorts of perils, Georgie began talking about going commercial with her river trips. She told them, "I'm going to take people down the river because, if I can get you dingalings through, I can take anybody down!"[3]

As a very determined, adventurous and innovative woman, Georgie began tying together Army surplus rafts left over from World War II. She had two goals: 1. To make a boat that would not flip; 2. To bring as many people as possible down through this remarkable landscape. Finally, she developed a huge raft that could carry 40 people and all their supplies and remained right side up even through Lava Falls!

At her 81st birthday party, someone asked, "Georgie, will you ever get married again?" Her reply was that if she could find a man who got her as excited as going over Lava Falls, you betcha she'd marry him! And, you know what? She never did marry again.[3]

In 1955, two thrill seekers, Bill Beer and John Daggett, told other River Runners that the stories were ridiculous about it being so difficult to run the river. They said that they could run the entire Colorado in life vests, and they did. Bill later said, "It's the most fun I ever had with my clothes on!"[3]

RED ROCK
CATHEDRAL

red rocks,
vertical cliffs
mirrored on
water glass—

I glide
in my vessel
on the water
as an artisan
slicing vast
pieces of
windowpane
for a red rock Cathedral
which sits on
the eternal green river.

The picture on the previous page shows the deepest section of the river at 80 to 100 feet; furthermore, the spirit of the river runs deep and clear within us as we continue to be amazed.

Beaver, the largest mammals to live in this part of the canyon, have abandoned their nests in these grass roots, but still live in this section of Glen Canyon.

As we round the bend, on the right we are reminded of an old Native American legend describing earlier ancestors to visit the river.

THE LEGEND OF THE TOROWEAP
(Paiute word for long valley)

As the legend goes, there was a very popular chieftain who ruled extremely well. He taught his people to fish and to hunt. He fell in love with a lovely maiden—their love was great, and the lovers lived happily. They ruled very well together and the people loved her as well.

The tribe prospered. However, the day came when the love of his life went away from the Chief to live with The Great Spirit. The Chief grieved and grieved. Nothing was the same. Actually, the entire tribe began to suffer. The chief was not able to rule as he had before, and his people became unruly. Hunting was not good, accidents happened, and generally, everyone was very unhappy.

Finally, the Chief went to the Great Spirit and said that if he could only see his true love again - even for just a day - he would be able to go on and be himself again, returning to his past efficient self. After much pleading, the Great Spirit agreed.

"Yes, I will grant your request," he said. "Go to the place just after the great bend in the Great River before it runs straight as an arrow. A place in the rock will open and your

love will come to you there. You may have one day together - only one day. Then, you must return to your people and rule as you did before. But remember, you only have one day, and must never return to that place again."

The Chief was delighted and did as he had been told. Rushing to the river, flushed with anticipation, he rounded the bend in the river. Mysteriously, the crevice in the cliff opened, and the Chief's love came forth from the rock. They embraced and spent a full day rejoicing in their reunion. Reluctantly, they parted at the end of the day, and the chief went back to his people. He was certain he could now go on.

At first, he continued as he had before, his memories of their reunion sustaining him. Eventually, however, his pain returned, and he yearned to see her once more. In the end, the Chief rushed to the bend in the river. Once again, as he rounded the bend, his love magically appeared from the cliff. However, this time, when she turned to face him, as soon as he reached out and placed his hand on her shoulder, they both immediately turned to stone.

Here's a little help, now you can see where they are.

As we leave the lovers on the cliff behind us, we come into the Two-Mile Stretch, so named because it is two miles from the canyon wall behind us to the one ahead. Five-Mile Stretch (on Lake Powell) is another straight section of river in the Glen Canyon National Recreation Area.

A freshwater lens of limestone is depicted in the picture on the right. Eons ago, a pool of water here eventually dried and lithified into the limestone layer you see here. These layers contain plentiful evidence of life through the fossil layer. Actually, the Colorado Plateau is one of the world's richest sources of fossils.

As we travel, we watch the walls of the canyon for shadows, since this is the best way to spot elusive birds such as Golden Eagles.

We also have Osprey, which like to dive for trout. According to David Herlocker, a wildlife expert on enature.com, the osprey has the highest success ratio, 60%, in catching its prey.

Of course, we have the elegant Great Blue Heron, leisurely pushing the warm air with his broad wings. The Great Blue Herons below have variations in plumage according to John R. Spence, PhD., from the National Park Service at the Glen Canyon Recreation Area. He stated that individual Great Blue Herons could vary significantly in the coloring of their feathers due to many factors.

We also see many Mallards along the way. Mallards are the most abundant species of duck in the world with over 10 million in North America and similar numbers in other parts of the world. Mallards seem to acclimatize to civilization quite well and have been known to nest in flowerbeds, by front doors, and even under gas meters.

If you should happen to see three, four, five or more birds about the size of Golden Eagles, they are probably Turkey Vultures. Golden Eagles are very territorial (each mated pair's territory is approximately 100 square miles) and will kill other eagles invading their territory.

At this point, our trip would not be complete without the ever-present raven. Actually, the raven is quite an interesting and talented bird. Most of us are not aware of some of his talents. Below, you will find a unique, true story about a raven.

The Raven Story

Vacationing up on Lake Powell at the back of Last Chance Canyon, I heard a goose honking. Not being the migration time for geese, I was curious. For quite a while, I searched the canyon walls to locate where the goose was sitting. Finally, I spotted the noisy creature. But, to my surprise, it was NOT a goose! Far up on a narrow ledge was a common black raven honking his heart out.

When I told my father about the incident, he said, "Yes, Ravens can imitate other sounds as well as crows. We had a crow out on my Aunt Pearl's farm. That crow could actually imitate Aunt Pearl calling the dog. When the crow would call, 'Dig-ger...Dig-ger,' the dog would come running! Of course, it was a real sideshow when the postman came. The dog would go out to the old dirt road and bark like crazy at the postman...

...and the crow would go out to meet the mailman as well, arch his back, spread out his wings, raise the feathers on his neck, jump up and down and bark, "WOOF, WOOF, WOOF!"

In the 1920's, the government was going to put what later became Hoover Dam along this section of the river. What you see here (below), on opposite sides of the river in the middle of the Two-Mile Stretch, is the reason why they decided not to. Where the sandstone has formed in vertical layers (a geologic structure referred to as jointing) is a left lateral slip strike fault, and they didn't want the dam slipping, striking and falling!

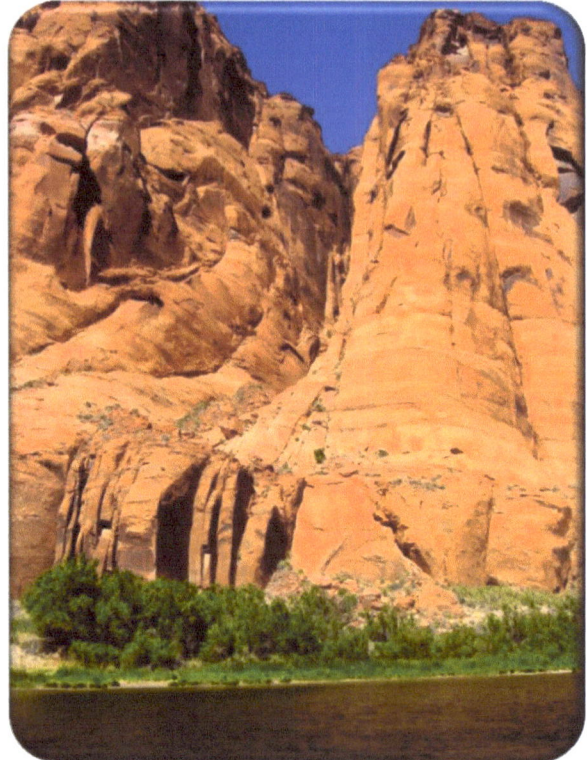

Right is the entrance to Waterholes Canyon, which is the last side canyon of Glen Canyon that was not filled with water after the dam was built. There is a little bridge about three miles South of Page on Highway 89, which crosses Waterholes. With a permit from the Navajo Tribe and some ropes, one can hike it down to the river.

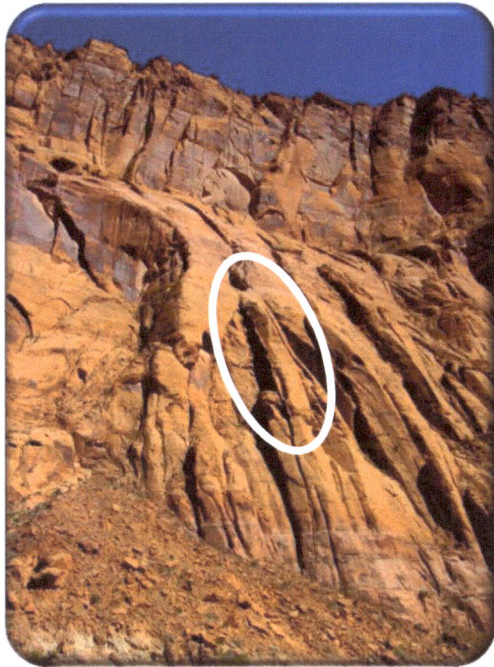

Finger Arch, left, looks like a big refrigerator handle

Hisslop's cave, below, was named because J. Hisslop carved his name into the back wall of this alcove. Hisslop was with a group in 1889 including Robert Stanton that had a plan to build a railroad through the Glen and Grand Canyons to provide transportation for gold from Colorado to the California Coast.

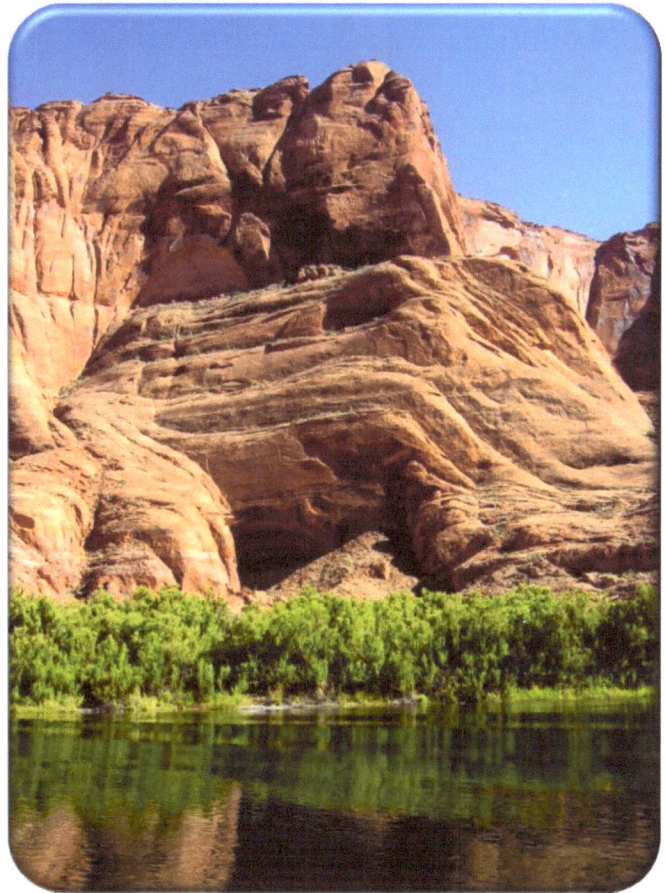

Later, Stanton returned to Glen Canyon to pursue his golden dream. Many people tried to get the powder gold out of Glen Canyon; however, the gold is a fine powder that is next to impossible to separate from the rock. One group earned only $66.96 in three months, and even back then that was not much money.[2]

The arrow on the left points out all that is left of the Stanton Mining Road. This photo also shows Cave Canyon, a box canyon where the outlet here is the only exit or entrance to the canyon. Remember the Westerns you've seen when someone gets chased into a box canyon to trap them?

31

And on the right, you can see Poison Rock. One drop from that and you're dead!

On the left is where we also begin seeing the Kayenta Sandstone. The Kayenta layer is the foundation for Rainbow Bridge on Lake Powell, which Howard Taft dedicated in 1910 as a national monument.

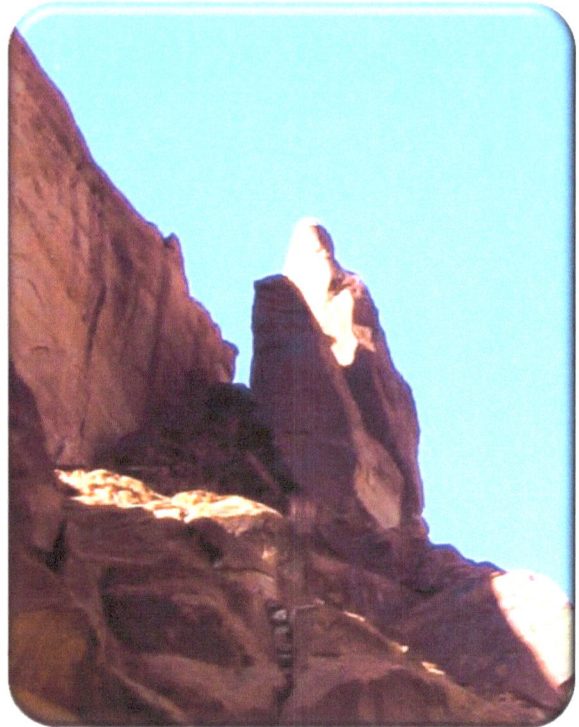

This bend of the river is the geologic beginning of Marble Canyon, which is 65 miles long. During Powell's 1871 expedition, a young cartographer and artist, Frederick Dellenbaugh, proclaimed that he could hike to the top of the sand dune ahead in half a day. Well, two and a half days later, he reached the top and fired Powell's pistol. It took exactly 24 seconds for the echo to come back. Each successive time that he fired the gun, it again took exactly 24 seconds for the report to return. Powell decided to call the peak above the sand dune, Echo Peak (2,600 feet high), which is actually part of a fault line named Echo Peak Fault Line. Because it is a fault line with one side of the fault grinding against the other uplifted layer, all the ground up rock and sand, which you see here, marks the area.

Notice how the canyon appears to be a totally different as we round the bend, which marks the beginning of what Powell named Marble Canyon. Powell felt that he was actually seeing marble, which was one of his few mistakes. As you can see, the cliffs are getting higher and higher as we journey southward.

Once we turn this next corner we will be back in civilization again. So I say farewell here at "Good-bye Rock." Only you and I know that this is "Good-bye Rock" because I named it and now I am telling you.

GOOD-BYE ROCK

The Colorado River blesses my soul; so, in leaving, I would like to leave you with my blessing:

May you be blessed with eyes
that see the prince or princess in the bulgy-eyed frog.

May you be blessed with ears
that hear the cleansing of a mountain stream
in your own tears.

May you be blessed with hands
that give the magic healing of touch.

And may you be blessed with voices
that sing even, in the rain.

After rounding the bend from Good-Bye Rock, we are at Lee's Ferry where powder gold is found in the sandstone and Chinle shale at Lee's Ferry (see photo on page 33), but is so fine that normal methods (panning and sluicing) do not work to extract the gold. Actually, the fine gold would just float on top of the water and float away.

Finally, a gold prospector named Charles Spencer decided to bring in a steamboat to bring coal down from the Warm Creek coal mine to fuel his new, fancy gold mining equipment. Indeed, it seemed a good idea because the paddle wheeler could operate in only two feet of water.

However, the boat only made two trips because it used as much coal to travel up and down the river as it could carry. After two years, Spencer abandoned both the ship and the effort to find gold here because it was just not profitable. The object you see above is the boiler from the steamboat - The Charles H. Spencer.

At Lee's Ferry this is one active Great Blue Herons' nests. Mama is tending this one.

Finally, we arrive at our destination the dock at Lee's Ferry, with the Vermillion Cliffs in the distance. Eleven Condors were released here in 1996. As of November 2010 there were 384 adult Condors in existence in the world today with 73 living in the wild in Arizona. The Peregrine Fund keeps track of them all including where they were born and how they were raised; they also keep records of how, where and when they die.

The first documented visit to this crossing was made by Padres Escalante and Dominguez on their journey in 1776 to find a route from Santa Fe, New Mexico, to Monterey, California. They descriptively named it "San Benito Salisipuedes," or "Get Out If You Can."

John D. Lee, a Mormon pioneer, settled Lee's Ferry in 1871. Mormons used what was called the Honeymoon Trail to access the ferry, cross the river and continue their trip to get married in the temple in St. George, Utah. Following Lee's execution for his role in the Meadow Mountain Massacre, his wife, Emma, ran the ferry for a few years before the Latter

Day Saints Church sent other families to run the ferry until 1928. That year, a horrible accident occurred at this site when a Model T Ford and three people went into the river. Following this mishap, the ferry was abandoned. For eight months, visitors to the area had to travel over 800 miles to cross the Colorado before the Navajo Bridge was opened in 1929.

The picture below is the current launching site and dock at Lee's Ferry.

So, it is here that we leave you. We wish you many opportunities to use your imagination and once again "run the river" with us. You'll feel humbled by majestic cliffs, ponder the wonder of an eagle's flight, delight in the memory of trout in the clear water, and have had "Colorado" written on our hearts. Certainly, we will take much with us from this enchanted land.

Have you decided why you came? And have you decided whether or not we have affected the river more than it has affected us? How has it affected you?

NOTES

1. Powell, John Wesley, *The Exploration of the Colorado River and Its Canyons,* page 260. London, England, Penguin Group, Inc., 2003.

2. Video: "River Runners of the Grand Canyon," Don Briggs Productions, Sausalito, California.

3. Westwood, Richard E., *Woman of the River*, page 38. Logan, Utah, Utah State University Press, 1997.

4. Mathis, Aliyson, *An Introduction to Desert Varnish* (with a copy of the technical report "Rock Varnish" by Dorn and Oberlander) in Glen Canyon NRA headquarters library.

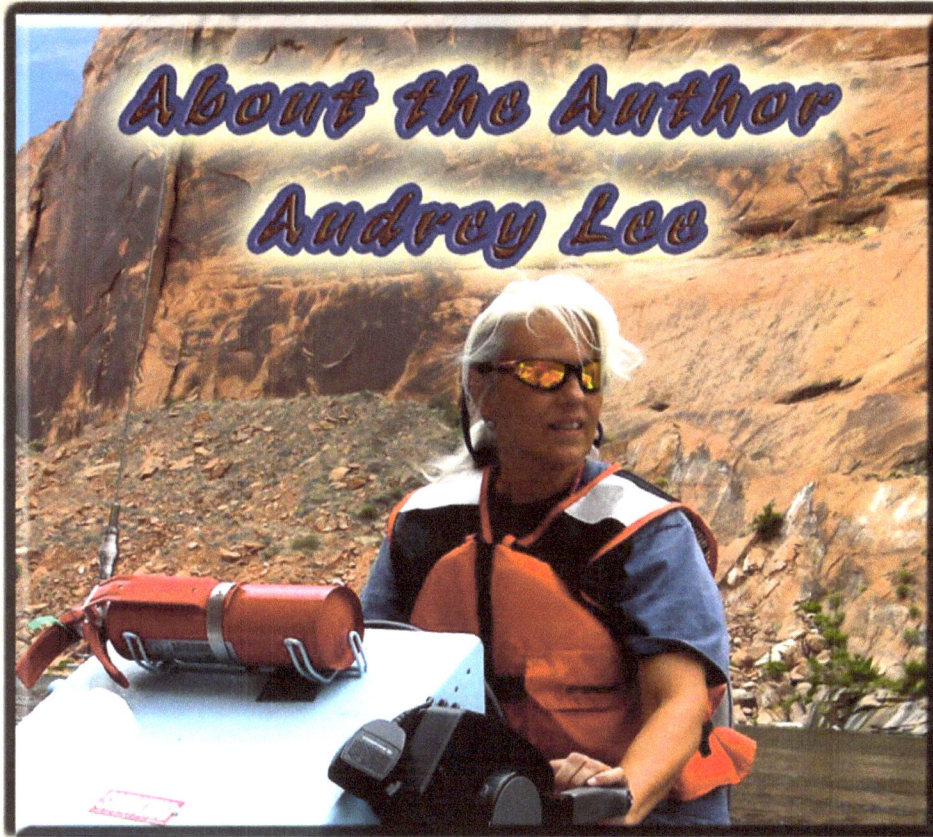

About the Author
Audrey Lee

Write "Colorado" on your heart by taking a realistic guided tour down the River with Audrey Lee, accomplished author, artist and pilot. Audrey ran the river for three years and worked on Lake Powell for another two years.

Experiencing the emerald green water and breath-taking vistas will bring you to a red rock cathedral that surpasses any man made structure on earth.

www.ingramcontent.com/pod-product-compliance
Lightning Source LLC
LaVergne TN
LVHW072107070426
835509LV00002B/60